MY JOURNEY BECOMING

H.E.R.

HEALING, ELEVATING, RELEASING

40 DAYS OF REFLECTION & INSPIRATIONAL POEMS

TIFFANY MCCLURE

3G Publishing, Inc.
Loganville, Ga 30052
www.3gpublishinginc.com
Phone: 1-888-442-9637

First published by 3G Publishing, Inc. September, 2023.

ISBN: 9781941247501

Printed in the United States of America

Contents

I was sitting here wondering how I would spend my
  40th birthday
Then here comes God revealing it in His own way
Normally I would take a trip
Or have a dinner or party to take a little sip
This year happens to be a little bit different
Especially when I reflect on my past to the current
This situation I wasn't expecting outside of my norm
But I said God I'll trust You as I am Your charm
God totally set me up for this birthday to come
I never dreamed of this day to come
He started showing me signs over a year ago
And gradually gave me the pieces and they begin to grow
I always knew 40 was a very symbolic number
Just as a pickle symbolic to a green cucumber
I was hesitant at first about reaching this milestone
Now I'm ready to embrace as I'm typing on my phone
I'm ready for the blessings that God has for me
Forever following His way as though I cant see
My confidence is at an all time high
Answering His will got me feeling strong and ready to fly!
I won't attempt anything moving forward without Him
Doing it on my own will cause my light to dim

I hope these words are encouraging to you
As I shared from my heart what's known to be true.
Just one of these poems a day
I hope to inspire you in such a special way!

Romans 8:28- And we know that in all things God works for the good of those who love him, who [a] have been called according to his purpose.

Daddy words would never express
How I endured the pain and stress
Of how I felt when you left and went away
Riding pass your home on numerous times that day
I knew it was past your time to be home
But my cousins told me "girl your daddy is grown"
I remember the next morning the loud banging on the door
I jumped up as it was the neighbor named Ms. Moore,
Screaming and yelling saying they think they had found
Walt in the car
I waited patiently at my aunt's like a little star
I became restless and then I said Toya "let's go"
As we walked around the road the fear begin to grow
When we walked upon the scene
It all felt just like a very bad dream
Watching them pull you from the car
Created a large wound and not just a scar
I wanted to breakdown, I wanted to yell,
I didn't know what to do, as if I was locked up in jail
Daddy you spoiled me tremendously
Since you been gone I've missed you immensely
I wrote my first poem at the age of 15
And I really thought it was a dream
I wrote a poem just for your obituary that was never seen
Because they didn't like me and thought I was your queen
Pops, you know how much you meant to me
And I know just what I meant to you
As you even celebrated my birthday every year too
This year is a special birthday dedicating this book to my
father who is no longer here
Coming from your baby girl Nussie your darling dear

I always struggle on most birthdays
Normally mad or sad wanting the day to go by fast
I know this is not how you would want me to be
As every birthday you always celebrated me
I celebrate you this 40th birthday wearing a smile as a start
For I will ALWAYS carry you deep in my heart!

2 Corinthians 6:18- I will be a Father to you,
and you will be my sons and daughters,
says the Lord Almighty.

A Moment to Breathe

Stop and take a moment to breathe the fresh air
Give all your troubles to God, to the one whom care
He is the one that gives you life each and everyday
So enjoy His nature in each and every way
Watching the sun rise when it comes up o so bright
Sit back and relax it's such a beautiful sight
Yes God created the heaven and the earth
With that in mind always know your worth
He knew you before your mother even gave birth
You was a bundle of joy brought to this earth
Continue to breathe and let go of the stress
Put it in Gods hand for He will handle the rest
You may need to take a brisk walk outside
When you have so many feelings bundled up inside
Again stop and take a moment to breathe
As you may find it even helpful to read
A breath of fresh air, A breath of fresh air
No more worries for we are in His care!

Exodus 14. 13 - Moses answered the people, "Do not be afraid. Stand firm and you will see the deliverance the Lord will bring you today. The Egyptians you see today you will never see again.

Too Heavy to Carry

When the weight of life seems to heavy to carry
You must take some weights off to bury
Sometimes the weight seems to weigh us down
We have to shake it off when there is no one around
Remember He would never put more on us than we can bare
Although we want to scream and possibly pull our hair
He never said it would be easy
Yes, sometimes in life things will get a little breezy
Although it may feel o' so heavy
But remember God built us tough like a Chevy
So don't you waiver and don't you bend
Gods got you until the very end!

1 Peter 5:7 - Cast all your anxiety on him because he cares for you.

I Never Imagined

My life turning around and feeling so trapped in
Feeling depressed thinking I'd never win
Married so early at the age of only twenty
Three months later my life turned around and begin to get
   gloomy
As I called his phone numerous times from work
I was getting no answer and thought he was acting like a
   jerk
Before taking my break I tried calling one more time His
friend answered and I could hear the crying
Saying my husband had got shot and he didn't know what
   to do
Then I begin to panic as I didn't know if it was true
Just praying and hoping everything wasn't true
He was rushed immediately to ICU
My colleagues begin to panic as they didn't want me to
   drive
So, Charlene hopped in the car and took me for a ride
He ended up paralyzed from his chest on down
The fear arose not being able for him to move around
I didn't know the cause as it didn't matter to me
I just wanted him well that's all I could see
Still trying to embrace every moment we shared
Keeping him uplifted because I really cared
It didn't matter to me that my husband was in a wheelchair
Still trying to keep him going as we were still a pair
He didn't want to go the right way or have us together
   as a family
That's when depression set in for him as no one could see
Threatening his life right before my eyes
It became a cycle I wouldn't tell you no lies

11

Keeping the faith and praying for a change
A couple years later things remained the same
With no one to relate with what I was going through
Then came "Diary of a Mad Black Woman" that I watched
    many times not just a few
As I was able to relate with what Helen was going through
It felt as if I was walking in her shoes...

*Eph 5: 15- 16- Be very careful, then, how you live—not as unwise but as wise, 16
making the most of every opportunity, because the days are evil.*

Him wanting to take an overdose while locking up in
  the room
I grabbed my son tight and covered him soon
We grew apart instantly with fussing and fighting
I almost lost custody of my son and that was so frightening
The authorities came out to inspect our home
I didn't panic I just stayed in my zone
While they were there, they found a freezer full of clothes
Destroyed with bleach as they had froze
Then there was a long knife sitting in his lap
I was glad they had identified it, as that was a wrap
I had to leave as that's what I chose
If not my baby would be with strangers those he didn't love
My son was in danger and the lady said, "ma'am you must leave"
I gathered our things quickly, and then we fleed
Praying things would change as there was a need
Not wanting to break up my little family
I gave it some time to hold on and to see
But things remained the same between us three
I remember him grabbing the wheel as we crossed the tracks
As I was scared as hell because I was under attack
It was all the drinking and the disrespect to me
You would think he would have chilled and let things be
Just keeping our minds on our perfect little family
He still wanted the things of the world
As I remained right by his side, his one and only girl
I realized there was nothing I had done
Besides taking care of him and our only son
Don't get me wrong we wanted for nothing

And for that made him great as he had a big heart
However we still grew apart
We are now friends to this day
And can call each other if we have anything to say
Sometimes individuals may go their own way
As it's best for them no matter what others has to say!

1 Corinthians 15:51 - Listen, I tell you a mystery: We will not all sleep, but we will all be changed

God kept Me

God kept you
God kept us
God is keeping me
God is keeping you
God is healing me
God is healing you
God is elevating me
God is elevating you
God is releasing me
God will release you too
We know God is keeping us
God will sustain us as well as maintain us
He will lead and direct our every path
We should look to Him and follow
Even through our pain and sorrow
Not just on special occasions or when we really have a need
But in all situations no matter the size of the seed
Stay encouraged
Don't give up, don't give in
God is the healer of all of our sin

*Psalm 121:1 - I lift up my eyes to the mountains –
where does my help come from?*

I declare I will have a heart of thanksgiving
Even while in the midst of needing a healing
Lord we have so much to be thankful for
Even when our hearts may be filled and feeling sore
Lord give us a thankful spirit especially thankful for You
For your presence around us and the relationship we
  have with You
We know that only You can heal in doing what You do
Father help us to remain humble and always showing
  kindness
Because only You can heal us from our blindness
Rather it's a physical, mental, or spiritual blindness
We trust You for all things our powerful Hiness
Heal us O'Lord as we trust You and abide in Your word
Thanking You in advance for healing us Your herd
We are forever grateful for our right now state
Father heal our hearts from negative thoughts even if
  it's hate
We thank You for everything even the things we
  consider small
Heal us from every stronghold and the unwanted wall
Help us to be thankful for the good days as well as the
  bad
Heal us O'Lord from our weary days when we are
  feeling down and sad
We thank You Lord for keeping us when we couldn't
  keep ourselves
Heal us O'Lord from the brokenness and pain that we
sometimes feel

Help us to be thankful knowing it's only temporary
    and a part of Your will
Heal us from our past that may try to hold us bound
Yet O'Lord we thank You for Your voice and sound
Heal us O'Lord from our physical pain and body ache
For we know we are healed by Your name sake!

*Psalm 119:71 - It was good for me to be afflicted
so that I might learn your decrees.*

We heard the saying, everything happens for a reason
What's taking place is only for a season
Don't get caught up in right now or even the past
For it's all for a purpose and this season will not last
It's only a life learning test
So give it to God for He got the rest
He will use you so He can get the glory
So don't you stress or even try to worry
It may be something deep and somewhat steep
Remember He is a jealous God so do not cheat
When you're going through situations, we should always
    look to God
Not looking to Tom, Tim, Derrick, or Todd
For they don't know what the purpose may be
Only God will have the answers for you and me
God knows the reason we go through what we go through
We will see the purpose if only we remain true
Many may come and many may even go
Some will serve a purpose that only God may know
No matter the purpose or the reason behind the scene
God will unfold it all no matter how long it may seem!

Romans 8:28- And we know that in all things God works for the good of those who love him, who [a] have been called according to his purpose.

God Knows my Heart

I'm so glad God knows my heart
No matter what it may have looked like from the start
God knew my every intention, and it sure wasn't to
    draw attention
Some could never understand my why
If I be honest I didn't either but I would just sigh
God would always convict me when I messed up
No one would never know as I tried to cover up
He was always there to carry me through
Even when others judged me and somethings wasn't true
I've never been big on explaining myself to others
Not even to my own sisters or brothers
Although, I may have done a lot of wrong
I continued praising God even through the storm
Many have judged me and some still do
Some may not know my heart as only God really do
Yes we all have to pay for the things we've done wrong
But that shouldn't shake your faith from still standing strong
Do not allow others to try and convict you
Have you feeling low just like they want you to
God is the only one who can and should judge
As others will try and even hold a grudge
My dear get on up and keep it moving
For it's God who knows your heart so keep on improving
I was left feeling low and thought I couldn't grow
However, I trusted God because He knew my heart and will
    have it to glow
Not for my own glory but just to share my story

Don't let anyone look down and try and frown

For you are Gods chosen one so still wear your crown
Remember God knows your heart , from the very start!

Luke 16: 15a -you are those who justify yourselves before men,
but God knows your heart.

God has a Plan

God has a plan for me and God has a plan for you
If only we trust God and know He will see us through
God has a plan although what we go through we might
  can't explain
We are a link in Gods divine unbreakable chain
If one is injured or hurt so are we all
Let us stand together so that we will not fall
Continue to stay focused on the overall goal
The goal of salvation for all of our souls,
Even when we can't see our way through
Remember God has a plan created just for you
God will always be here to keep us and sustain us
When you keep God first it will always be a plus
God has a plan and so whom shall we fear
Remember God has a plan and He is always near
God states, for I know the plans I have for you says
  Jeremiah 29:11, help us to follow your plan as it will lead
  us to the gates of heaven
Help us to trust Your plan although we may not know
  the details
Trusting You will fill our bodies from your ever flowing well
I pray that we will trust Your plan and give You the glory
Because of Your plan we will share our story
Help us to look to You and Your plan as You are our guide
We pray for a spirit of humbleness letting go of all pride
God You have a plan and You are our compass and source of
  direction
Keep us in Your word with a spirit of meditation
Let us lean not to our own understanding but in all our
  ways we want to acknowledge You
As You will continue to direct our paths help us to give a
  soft answer as it will turn away wrath

We know You are the answer to our problem, the solution
    to the equation
You are the sum to all of our problems added together
Because You have a plan for us that is forever
God has a plan for our increase in His divine timing and
    plan
God has a plan for our healing in his divine timing and plan
God has a plan for each of our lives
If only we trust Him and follow His word as it will keep us
    wise
I encourage you to follow Gods plan and not our very own
    because following our own can very much lead us wrong
Allow God to lead the way as He knows all
Even when we are about to fall. I can not say it enough,
    God has a plan for each one of us!
A plan to keep us
A plan to heal us
A plan to sustain us
A plan to maintain us
A plan to bring us out
A plan to take us higher
A plan to grow us
A plan to heal us from our hurt
A plan for our pain
A plan for our struggle
A plan even while in the rain
Remember, God has a plan
If only we remain his number one fan
God has a plan!!

*Jeremiah 29:11 -For I know the plans I have for you," declares the Lord, "plans
to prosper you and not to harm you, plans to give you hope and a future.*

Have you ever felt or knew that there was something special
    about you
No, you're not alone I had that same feeling too
I didn't know exactly what it was
I knew it was something special from up above
I wouldn't have known if I didn't remain close to the Lord
Now realizing He was shaping and molding me all from
    above
Don't look for a man or woman to bring out the best in you
Look to God because He already knows and doesn't need a
    clue
He created me, I'm not perfect but I'm just me
Trusting God as He is bringing out the best within me
I knew it was so much stored inside
I just kept going trying to lay back and hide
I was curious as to how it would come out of me
Now that I'm trusting God more I'm starting to see
I had to go through the process as He was fulfilling me
There was times in life when I wondered "Lord why me"
It's because He chose me, to inspire, encourage as He is
    elevating me
Although I know there is something special designed for
    me to do
I know I can't do it on my own without Gods help too
There is a calling on all of our lives,
Even the kids, the husbands, and the wives
Titles sometimes can mean nothing
If you don't trust God and His covenant
I learned to be content in whatever situation God placed
    me in

Not saying it was easy but He gave me the peace from
  within
We all were fearfully and wonderfully made
Let's embrace your speciality in Him like we're at a parade
You are special, you are kind, you are sweet, you are Gods
  special treat!

Psalm 139:13-For you created my inmost being;
you knit me together in my mother's womb.

O Ye of Little Faith

O ye of little faith,
All you need is the faith the size of a mustard seed
Put your faith in God as He will supply your every need
Although you may not know when or maybe how
God will bring it to pass and have you feeling like wow
Faith is believing the things that we can not see
But trusting that God will always set us free
Having faith without works is truly dead
So you must work and have God as the head
Although you can't see what lies ahead
That's the beautiful thing watching Him work as you are
   being led
Corinthians 13:13 shares and now these three remain
  faith, hope, and love, for the greatest of these is love
For without faith it is impossible to please Him that's above
Love must be sincere, and there should be only God whom
   we fear
For we walk by faith and not by sight
You just have to trust God with all of your might
Lean not to your own understanding for in all your ways
   submit to Him
For we are His children a very special gem
Have faith in God for His mercy endureth forever
When you have faith in God it shows you are very clever
Knowing God will not leave you now or never
Whoever has faith and believe in Him
Out of his belly shall flow rivers of living water from within
   them
God does answers prayers
In spite of the nay sayers

Romans 10:11 states whoever believes in Him will never be put to shame

Remember to have faith, hope, and love and trust in His name.

Matthew 17:20-21-He replied, "Because you have so little faith. Truly I tell you, if you have faith as small as a mustard seed, you can say to this mountain, 'Move from here to there,' and it will move. Nothing will be impossible for you."

Give and it shall be given unto you, good measures pressed down shaken together and running over, is Gods word even if you're older, we want to be a cheerful giver, that will also symbolize our faith as a believer, when we give from our hearts, God can bless us beyond the charts, giving not just our treasures but also our time, as our time is truly valuable and should be treated kind,

Gods word tells us where our treasure is there our heart is also, when we give from the heart there will be a blessing to follow, there is nothing too big or too small when we give to God, as long as we are giving our best of all, we should be inspired to pay our tithes, even bringing our offerings for there should be nothing to hide, when we give God will always have our back, so don't be stingy when you're digging in your little sack, what we make happen for others, God will make happen unto you, always trust Him and He will see us through, He will never leave the righteous begging for bread, for in Psalms 37:25 That's what he said, God has a blessing with your name on it, no matter your name just trust God and own it, where there is a will there will always be a way, you don't have to worry where you will stay, count it all joy it's a blessing to give, don't let your giving be in vain but according to His will, it can never hurt to be a blessing to one another, not just to your sister or even a brother, we are all connected in one way or another, and it may not be by a biological mother,

God can stretch our dollar much further than us, but remember you must always trust, just like He fed the multitude with only bread and fish, he can stretch anything according to your wish,

I encourage you to remain faithful in your giving, as you
will be blessed in your living, He promised us life and life
more abundantly, so don't just give thinking redundantly,
just know that I am blessed, you are blessed, and we are all
blessed, and when we give, God will give us the rest
It shall be given back unto you!
Help us to listen and give while we are on our life mission,
Remember God loves a cheerful giver, good measures
pressed down shaken together and running over!!!

Luke 6:38-Give, and it will be given to you. A good measure, pressed down, shaken together and running over, will be poured into your lap. For with the measure you use, it will be measured to you."

He Will Provide

When you think you don't have
Know God will provide
When you think there is no way through
God will provide
When you think you may not have quite enough
When you think you don't have the skill
God will provide
Even when you see no food in the pantry God will
provide, when your finanaces get
Cut God will still provide
Just always look to God for
He is right by your side
Don't be ashamed or feel you have to hide
For He is there with you, right there by your side
God will provide us with
The daily bread that we need
You don't have to beg and beg as that would be greed
God knows exactly how much we need
Even if it's a small amount the size of a seed
As God will continue to provide for us
Let us give to others for it is in God we trust
You don't have to look to others and begin to lust
God will provide
So in Him there you place your trust.

Phil 4:19- And my God will meet all your needs according to
the riches of his glory in Christ Jesus.

I speak more peace than confusion

I speak more smiles than frowns

I speak more loving than hating

I speak more giving than receiving

I speak more obedience than my own way

I speak more ups than downs

I speak more battles I'll give to You, vs me fighting

I speak more pleasure than pain

I speak more of Your will and not my own

I speak more living and not just existing

I speak more cheerful to give than to receive

I speak more faith than fear when in a battle

I speak more trust in You than rush in the
  process

I speak more of it will work out vs me having doubt

I speak more stability than imbalance

I speak more consistency than inconsistent

I speak being more on one accord than discrepancies

I speak more of You and less of me

I speak more things in order than out of order

I speak more speaking in turn than out of turn

I speak more God got this than I got this

I speak more having appreciation than being ungrateful

I speak more of Gods will than your own will

I speak more appropriate than inappropriate behavior

I speak more light shining bright than a dim light not shining

I speak more positive influence on others than negative
  influences

I speak bringing more positive energy to the table than
  negative

I speak being more of a motivation and inspiration than
    deterioration unto others
I speak more pouring into my cup than drinking from
    the cup, Lord I speak exceedingly abundantly life and
    favor!

John 10: 10- The thief comes only to steal and kill and destroy; I have come that they may have life, and have it to the full.

I drifted away in such a short period of time
He say I begin to talk aloud in my sleep
Saying "we not going to be long" while laying on the sheet
As I begin to fall asleep with him on my mind
It was only a fantasy dream about me and him
But he thought it was about I guess a guy named Tim
I have no clue who Tim is
As I was just tired from housekeeping and kids
He awakened me with anger
And I jumped as I thought I was in danger
I didn't know what was going on
But he say "something is wrong"
I had no clue what I said, I was sleep talking
But a few days later he gathered his bags and got to walking
Things were not what they seemed
Although it seemed real
I thought he would cool off and chill
I was so innocent and nothing made any sense
Even when I tried to explain, things only got more tense
I knew God had allowed all of this to happen
So I just chilled and allowed God to be my captain
I didn't know the answer to why God had allowed
But He wanted to see if I would trust Him and just follow
I thought it was all a joke and would soon fade away
But there were hours, weeks, and then months that rolled
   away, with nothing to say
Normally it wouldn't seem to be this very long
But it was God that kept me mighty and strong
Truly not knowing how things would unfold
Just still trusting God until the end of the road
Holding things down and trying not to frown

Continuously thanking God for keeping me sound
Trying to stay obedient and focus so I may earn my crown!

2 Timothy 4:8- Now there is in store for me the crown of righteousness, which the Lord, the righteous Judge, will award to me on that day – and not only to me, but also to all who have longed for his appearing.

He left Me

Just when he left me
That's when my eyes begin to open so I can see
I didn't understand why
But God was there during my cry
God allowed the situation to happen
He removed all the lying or shall I say cappin
When he left me there was a peace that was upon me
A peace I couldn't explain but it was just like I was free
I knew that without a doubt God was in the midst
That's how I continued even though I longed for a kiss
God knew just what I needed and when I needed it most
I was lost at first up looking like a ghost
I said I won't rush the process I'll wait patiently a mist
I didn't want to rush and take any risks
It's important to not be anxious about anything
Whether a man, woman, or even a friend
When you know God is in control
You can always relax and give God all of your soul
I had to trust God even more when OG left me
I was like the branches just sitting on the tree
As they were clipped off piece by piece
Yet the tree still stood firm
As God protected me from all of the harm
I didn't know what the outcome would be
Yet I trusted God because he allowed him to leave me
This wasn't the first time OG left me
On a few other occurrences possibly more even three
I couldn't trust God halfway and not trust Him for all
I had to give him the situation I mean ALL
When he left me I was really in disbelief

Yet it was real and somewhat of a relief
I couldn't understand what was taking place
However I trusted God while in the race
I invited God totally in my home and in all of my space
I wanted to handle the situation myself on several occasions
But God said stand still and then I went on vacation
A vacation that drew us even farther apart
Having both of our emotions racing off the chart
Although earthly man OG left me
God was right there with me
OG's presence was missing at times in the home
But that allowed more of God's love to be shown
I didn't need man as it became a distraction
Yet I had a need to keep my eyes on God for His satisfaction

Joshua 1:9-Have I not commanded you? Be strong and courageous. Do not be afraid; do not be discouraged, for the Lord your God will be with you wherever you go. "

Well, well, well, what do I say
I will start with let go and let God have His way
Let go of the anger
As it can lead to danger
Let God have His way and stop trying to fix it
Let it go and allow God to build or rebuild it
Let go of trying to figure it out
Because God has already worked it out
Sometimes I know its hard to let it go
But when you let go
   you let God allow you to grow,
We keep trying to put our hand in it
But let it go and let God win it!
We keep trying to be stubborn as a horse
But let it go and allow God to be your source
We have to let God and trust Him in all things
For He is King of Kings!

Exodus 14:14-The Lord will fight for you; you need only to be still."

Do not Worry

Do not worry about tomorrow and what it may bring
Just rejoice on this day and feel free to sing
For tomorrow has enough troubles of its own
So focus on today, and today all alone
Tomorrow will always take care of itself
Worrying about tomorrow can lead you to sudden death
Do not be anxious for tomorrow
As it can lead us to live in horror
Tomorrow is beyond all of our control
So just relax and watch how it unfolds,
Thanking the Lord daily for the gift of bread
We can depend on Him knowing we will be fed
Lord help us to not worry and lean not to our own
understanding

Yet trusting You and still here withstanding
God has everything already worked out
You will soon see it and be able to shout
Everything works together for our good in the end
So don't you worry, you will have victory and win!

Matthew 6:34 - Therefore do not worry about tomorrow, for tomorrow will worry about itself. Each day has enough trouble of its own.

Trust God

I know it's sometimes easier said than done
For we should trust God for He is the only one
We say we trust Him and still try to do it on our own
Causing frustration and possibly cause us to moan
We have to give it to Him, in God whom we trust
Placing the problem in His hands will always be a must
If we trust Him for one thing we should trust Him
for them all
He has the say so with the last and final call
When trusting in God you can never go wrong
Trusting in God will keep you mighty and strong
His word tells us to put trust in no man
God will never deceive us as man always can
As man will sometimes let us down
Have us looking sad and even carrying a frown
Just know God is able to do just what He say
We shouldn't want to have it any other way!

*Proverbs 3:5 - Trust in the Lord with all your heart
and lean not on your own understanding...*

Just Follow

Sometimes we may wonder on which way to go
Let me encourage you to take a deep breath before you proceed to go
We may look all around for some direction to follow
Continuing trying to search and still feeling hollow
As you trust God, He will direct your path
Acknowledge exactly how you feel don't try
to cover and mask
Allow Him to lead and guide your way
Although it may not be clear but trust what He say
The road may have you feeling in an unfamiliar place
Feeling confused just trust God and put a
smile on your face
God will direct you to where He will have you to go
Just hold on tight and get ready for this show
You may not understand it when it all starts to form
But He will never lead you to any type of harm
Continue to remain obedient and listening to His voice
He granted us a free will to make our very own choice
God will never leave you or forsake you
As you trust in Him, He will forever guide you through
Open your eyes and your ears to what He has to say
And He will see you through each and every day!

*Proverbs 3:6-in all your ways submit to him,
and he will make your paths straight.*

39

They say your word is all that you have
Use it wisely to build the morale
When your word is not enough
It's because someone has lost trust
Believing in your words and what you have to say
Then they don't come true because something get in the way
Yes, sometimes things do come up
But it begins a pattern as things start to corrupt
Wishing we could believe everything you say
Again, there has been trust lost along the way
Your words now only hold little to no weight
It just appears as a pattern of a common trait
Looking back on all the words you shared
We believed them all because we really cared
Listening to your words then comes an excuse
Then we realized listening was of no good use
The things you say can get our hopes up high
It not coming to pass, then it appears it was just a lie
It's hard to build trust when your words aren't true
Even when it's things just about me and you
Your words had me excited for a lot of big things
They never came to pass just only in a wishful dream
I may can't hold to all my words I say
But I'm not just saying words along the pathway
I try to fulfill the words that I say
Acting upon them to bring them to play
Speaking words aloud with good intent
Can have a positive outcome that was really meant
With trust, your word can be so powerful
But when it's only words they can mean so little too
Please don't just say things just to be talking

Because when it don't line up trust begin to walking
People begin to listen at what you say
Just to be let down then they go and pray
After multiple times, it's no longer a mistake
Soon they will realize and then awake
You have created the reason no one trust in you
Be careful with your words and try to keep them true!

*Proverbs 18:21 - The tongue has the power of life and death,
and those who love it will eat its fruit.*

Temptation

Temptation will always try to rise
Just stand strong and continue to abide
The flesh will have you feeling weak
But trust in the Lord for you will not be beat
It's a struggle we all have fought or even fight
Temptation come strong, forcing with all its might
The devil know all of our weaknesses
Yet give them all to God in meeknesses
Don't allow the flesh to win over the Spirit
For the flesh is weak and the Spirit is willing
We must crucify the flesh every single day
Trying to avoid temptation and to do it Gods way
Temptation will have you feeling pretty good
Doing what you want and not as you should
Yet can have you all tangled up and misunderstood
Don't fulfill your wants by giving in to temptation
Yet feed the Spirit, with His word and meditation
Temptation can have you battling within yourself
Just trying to score again to satisfy self
Temptation is a trick of the enemy
As Only God is our remedy
Temptation is like feeding the flesh
I'm encouraging you to not get in that mess
Temptation is only a temporary satisfaction
But turning to God is a beautiful attraction
Only God can fill the void that you're trying to fill
Rather it be curiosity or just wanting a thrill
Temptations can be a hard battle to fight
But give it to God with all of your might … you can
   and will overcome temptation!!!

Proverbs 4: 14: 15-Do not set foot on the path of the wicked or walk in the way of evildoers. Avoid it, do not travel on it; turn from it and go on your way.

<h1 style="text-align:center">Better Days</h1>

Sometimes we are going through looking for better
Continue to hang in there inspite of the weather
Better days are indeed coming to you
Stay true unto God and He will remain true unto you
The clouds may sometimes hang a little low
But soon they will move for this I know
The sun is going to rise and then shine
He has spoken and said "child you are mine"
This is only a test you are going through
God never promised us that each day will be bright
However, doing it with Him is worth every fight
The battles that we endure may be hard to carry on
But trust in the Lord for you have already won!

*1 Corinthians 2:9 - However, as it is written: What no eye has seen,
what no ear has heard, and what no human mind has conceived" –
the things God has prepared for those who love him –*

We have the victory
So we should live each moment like we are free
Free from guilt, and free from pain
You have the victory with God, for He is gain
With God we will have more wins
Confessing to Him and trying to flee from our sins
Greater is He that is in us than we ourselves
We just have to reach for the victory off of God's shelves
For we can't do it on our very own
We need God to let it be shown
We are nothing without Him
Just like a tire with no rim
Therefore we can go anywhere and be anything we want to be
We just need the faith the size of mustard seed
And trust God and allow Him to lead
He will take you to anywhere or anything
If you only express your very need
I should overcome, you shall overcome, we shall overcome
No matter what we're going through or where we come from
Our past shouldn't stop us from moving into the future
For we are no longer babes in Christ just older and maturer!
The battle is not yours
But it's the Lord's.

Deuteronomy 20:4-For the Lord your God is the one who goes with you to fight for you against your enemies to give you victory.

A New Creation

A new creation in Him we all can be
As old things and old ways pass away that's when we can see
We may not do the things we used to do
Because the more you're in Christ the more you become new
We will always be a work in progress
So don't think you will be perfect, that will only cause stress
For all have sinned and fallen short of his glory
But when you're new, feel free to share your story
No one can judge you no matter big or small
Because when you're in Christ, He makes the call
We all fall short each and everyday
We have to strive in our own way
We must deny ourselves and the things that we want
Doing what God says as He appoint
When you become new more will try to attack you
But God got you as long as you remain true
Becoming new is like a caterpillar transforming
Becoming a butterfly in the sky looking and roaming
It had to go through the complex process
Before it can display its beautiful success!

2 Corinthians 5: 17 - Therefore, if anyone is in Christ, the new creation has come: [a] The old has gone, the new is here!

When you Listen

When you listen to what they really have to say
Then you can get down dirty and maybe even play
Being able to listen even when you really don't want to
If she is not expressing it, it is only creating pain on the
inside
Just listen to her even if it's just for a little while
We all have our perceptions and different views
However, it doesn't make me any smaller than you
When you sit back and listen you can gain so much
   more knowledge
Asking her questions and getting to see the others logic
When she keeps it all inside it begins to instantly build up
As she needs to get it out before getting fed up
Not knowing her actions then she's yelling out shut up
When she is quiet, try to find out what's really going on
You never know there could be something going wrong
Just listen even if you don't want to hear it
For she will feel better just because she vented
It will make her think she's living on top of the world
Even when she's feeling like a stinking little turd
When you listen she will gain more respect for you
And if you don't then she will start to stray away from you
Listening draws you closer to each other
Just like a son being with his mother
Yes, listening takes both patience and time
But it's worth a try as communication is prime!

James 1:19-20- My dear brothers and sisters, take note of this: Everyone should be quick to listen, slow to speak and slow to become angry, 20 because human anger does not produce the righteousness that God desires.

Healing

Dear my sister and brother in Christ
Let's direct our attention to the only one who is right
We can bring to Him all of our burdens and needs
Because after all He can supply everything indeed
No matter if the need is for healing
Let's look to Him because He is willing
No matter what the healing may look like
God has all the power to make everything alright
We can't heal ourselves on our very own
Sometimes we may have to look to Him and moan
God knows and sees our all
When you need a healing just know there is only one to call
Sometimes we think we can do it on our own and that will
    make us fall
Remember to put all your trust in God for He can heal us all
There are different healing stages you may have to face
But if you remain in God, you are in the right space
Although we all may stand in the need
Just continue to pray and always read
For His word will always see us through
Even when we think we don't have the strength to go and do
We know that God holds all healing power in His hand
Therefore, we must trust God and really not man
For God already has His plan
We must remain still and only stand
Always standing on Gods promises as He has a healing for all us
No matter the healing we may need just look to God and trust
In spite of what the situation may look like
Help us to never fear or even fright
No matter what the doctor may say
Or even when our past may get in the way

Help us to only focus on what's happening today
And allow you to lead us through the way
For we don't know what tomorrow may hold
Yet that is far beyond our control
Father we will continue to share our stories that should be told
So, Father we come to you for all types of healing,
For there is no healing too big or too small
For we know that you can heal all!

Jeremiah 30:17-But I will restore you to health and heal your wounds, declares the Lord, because you are called an outcast, Zion for whom no one cares.

Free yourself from the things that have you bound
First be honest with yourself without making any sound
God already sees and of course He knows all
Free yourself first by acknowledging your fall
Facing it and allowing God to help you fix it
No one is perfect we all have made mistakes
Just don't waddle in it for His name sake
He will free you but first you must free yourself
Stop trying to hide it because you're only fooling yourself
Be honest with you for the truth will reveal itself
The word tells us the truth will set you free
Even when you're thinking no one is looking to see
You may only hide it for so long
Just know that hiding is not making you strong
You may do it behind closed doors
But be honest as if you're only doing chores
For all have sinned and fallen short of his glory
Free yourself first so then you don't have to worry!
It feels good!

Proverbs 6:3 - So do this, my son, to free yourself, since you have fallen into your neighbor's hands: Go — to the point of exhaustion — and give your neighbor no rest!

Patiently Waiting

How patiently are you waiting
Are you trusting and seeking God and yet still pacing
Are you reading and praying and yet still waiting
They that wait in the Lord shall renew their strength
Even when it seems hard not focusing on the time length
Remain patient as you continue to wait
As He will guide you walking you straight
God can hear your humble cry
Keep seeking His will or at least attempt to try
We don't know how long the wait may be
That's where our faith comes in for the things we cannot see
You will mount up with wings as eagles
For that is His word and not illegal
We shall run and not be weary; yet walk and never faint
Only trust Him and wait patiently on the Lord you my
   dear Saint!

Psalm 37:7 - Be still before the Lord and wait patiently for him: do not fret when people succeed in their ways, when they carry out their wicked schemes.

Grace

There is Grace
That comes from a very special place
Grace always given at the perfect time and space
Gods grace is sufficient for us
His grace and his mercy I trust
Not because we've been so good
But God giving us grace because only He would
After so many times trying to do it on our own
Yet there is Gods grace still being shown
Lord we are thankful for your grace
Although you're not here for us to see your face
O God we are grateful for all things
Knowing it comes from the King of all Kings
Grace is a gift that we don't deserve
Therefore we know it only comes from Him up above
Let's thank Him for His grace and His covering upon us
Knowing it could have been worse but yet He kept us
For by His grace we are saved by faith
It's even His Grace on today that we are awake!

2 Cor 12:9-10-But he said to me, "My grace is sufficient for you, for my power is made perfect in weakness." Therefore I will boast all the more gladly about my weaknesses, so that Christ's power may rest on me. 10 That is why, for Christ's sake, I delight in weaknesses, in insults, in hardships, in persecutions, in difficulties. For when I am weak, then I am strong.

Just One Day Away

It's ok to take a day away
A day for yourself no matter what others may say
A time for you to reflect and just refresh
Stop treating yourself like a stranger or a guest
We should love ourselves just as Christ love us
Self care is important and is a must
I found it hard being able to speak up and share how I feel
Sometimes it's not until I get away and start to keep things real
Let's try and focus on meditating both day and night
For His word in our heart will keep us just so right
Remember we will never be perfect in anyone's sight
The goal is to keep striving to doing what's right
Sometimes just one day away can help renew your mind
Just one day away if only for a little time
We get soo busy in everyday life
We forget about ourselves in being a mom and sometimes a wife
From work to church and family all abroad
Give yourself one day for I know this may be hard
But continue to give God the praise and trust in the Lord
Father your word tells us where two or three gather there
    You will be in the mist
Hear our prayer O'Lord as You are our shining bliss
Father we pray You have your way on this day
That we will trust You in all we do and say
Go before us and continue to lead the way
As we come with humble hearts to speak and to pray
Father we ask that You take us to a higher height
As we trust You with all of our might
We know this time is not by an coincidence
But we come together by your divine providence
So father we ask You continue to connect us together

Always seeking You now and forever
May each of us continue to let our light shine bright
Holding on to you as you shine our light
Let us not be focus just on us
but on everyone and teaching them to trust
Father we ask you continue to help us to obey,
Leading and following you every step of the way
As we refocus with just one day away

Matthew 11:28- Come to me, all you who are weary and burdened,
and I will give you rest.

Girl Get Up

Girl get up and and get out
Because God got you without a doubt
God has me and God has you
All you need to do is get up and remain true
Remain true to yourself as well as others too
Because God got his eyes on both me and you
It's ok if perhaps you may have fell
As long as you don't stay down with the possibility of going
    to hell
We all get weak and sometimes stumble
But the ultimate goal is to get up and remain humble
God didn't put you here to be alone
He is right here with us watching from the throne
Psalm 46:5 says, "God is within her", meaning her like you
    and me
She will not fall especially when you give God your all
It says God will help her at break of day
Girl you better get up and trust what God has to say!
We will trust everyone else and sometimes mess
Versus us getting on up and allowing God to take care of the rest
No weapon formed against me or you shall prosper
Because we are trusting God to lead us through
Let's count it all joy the good and even the bad
Because God plans for us will make the devil mad
God has a plan for both you and me
We just have to keep the faith although we can't see
Girl let us get up and let our light shine
Because we are Gods chosen one so let us not whine
I want to encourage you to carry God with you wherever
    you may go
So girl get on up and put on a show

Not for your glory but so God can glow
Remember we may stumble but His word say we will not fall
Let's get our mind right and give God our ALL
Not just this hour, or just today
but even when you feel low and think you may fall
It may not be as bad as it seems
Girl get up and go follow your dreams
I encourage you to write your vision and make it plain
Nothing is too hard for God even when it seems insane
Sometimes you are stretched, and even pulled
Girl you better get up and follow Gods rule
It may be difficult and sometimes challenging
It may even become a struggle
Girl get up because God got you covered
The devil may try to stop you and even try and block you
    but girl you better keep going and get on up because
    God got you!

Psalm 139:14 - I praise you because I am fearfully and wonderfully made; your works are wonderful, I know that full well.

It's Time to Flourish

For like a flower there is a time and season
Yet Gods timing is always for a reason
He has to take us through the process
So just hold on throughout the test even if it feels like
  a mess
We will know when its time
For He will give you a little clue since He is kind
Not too much and not too big
Just enough to get you going to plant a seed
God knows our every thought and of course our every need
You cannot flourish without nourishing your seed
Be obedient to His word and to His way
As you'll begin to grow day by day
Just like a baby you can't see them grow
But you can look back after an appointed time and say whoa
Growing sometimes causes aches and pains
Some days will be sunshine and others can be rain
We know a flower need water to grow
So the rain will help the seed that we began to sow
As she begin to flourish and bloom
You want to keep God surrounded in the room
The room she walks in, the room she speaks in
The room she fills and flourish from within
She will grow, as only God know
He know when and He know where
Just trust the process even when it seems rare
For God will always care!

Jeremiah 17:7-8-But blessed is the one who trusts in the Lord, whose confidence is in him. 8 They will be like a tree planted by the water   that sends out its roots by the stream. It does not fear when heat comes; its leaves are always green. It has no worries in a year of drought and never fails to bear fruit.

Love

What is love?
Love is a deep, tender, ineffable feeling of affection
When you truly love there are no limits or hesitation
Love will come and love will go
Don't get caught up in the way that loves flow
When you are truly loved you will always know
You want have any doubts or wonder if it should be so
Falling in love will not happen overnight
Always pray about it and you will know when the timing is right
Love is not physical or mental abuse
Neither is love a feeling of being misused
Love is pure, love is kind
When you love you should love with a Christ like mind
Love is patient, love is kind
Looking for true love you need to seek God for a sign
Love does not envy and it does not brag or boast
Love is like strawberry preserve on some buttered toast
True love you don't have to force or press
You don't have to continue to struggle or be in stress
With love you can tell the rest and feel it deep down in
　your chest!

1 Corinthians 13:4-8a-Love is patient, love is kind. It does not envy, it does not boast, it is not proud. It does not dishonor others, it is not self-seeking, it is not easily angered, it keeps no record of wrongs. Love does not delight in evil but rejoices with the truth. It always protects, always trusts, always hopes, always perseveres. Love never fails. But where there are prophecies, they will cease; where there are tongues, they will be stilled; where there is knowledge, it will pass away.

The Power He Holds

A man is so strong and yet so powerful
He don't realize the strength and influence he carry
Sometimes not even after he marrry
Men were created to be the head
However, sometimes it's hard to follow when you don't know
    where you're being led
Trust Him and follow Him if He has God as his head
If his actions align with what he has said
Give it a try and follow him for he is the head
Continue to seek God first and trust Him as you're being led
Women were made to be a "help mate"
Not to takeover and be the "everything mate"
She doesn't want to do it all
But she will try before she watches everything fall
For some women it's hard to sit back
Especially when she has waited and can see there is a lack
A woman wants to obey God and just sit back and submit
Just to be that "help mate", what God created her with
Yes, God created Adam the man whom He created first
And it was Eve, the woman who bit the apple and started the
    curse
However, that still leaves man the head so no man should
    never take their eyes off God
Even when it gets hard like trying to untangle a cord
When a man is supposed to be leading and there is no one
    following, he is only taking a walk
Especially when his actions don't align with his talk

Continue to cover him in prayer
Continue to trust God
Cover your home in prayer
Continue to trust God and He will see you through!

2 Corinthians 5: 17 - Therefore, if anyone is in Christ, the new creation has
come: [a] The old has gone, the new is here!

Something about the gut feeling we call intuition
It's like not knowing but being shown a vision
That feeling of thinking something isn't right
We try to move forward, and it's right before our sight
All the signs can be right before you
Instead you'll ignore hoping it's not true
Allowing time to pass away
And believing and hoping it's another way
There were times when it was right there
But I ignored as if it was just a glare
I would look away, and continue to search and stare
Some days were too hard and seemed I couldn't bare
They'd share a story trying to cover up and keep me unaware
Sometimes I would dig and ask many questions just to hear
what the outcome would be
Then comes another story or excuse given unto me
God continued to keep His hands all around me
His smile resting upon me although I could not see
He had set me free and then came a cheer
Which had me smiling from ear to ear
That intuition did not lead me wrong
I just ignored it for too long
God will never leave His people to be blind
Just keep your eyes open as He will show you the sign
Always remaining humble and trying to stay kind!

1 King 3:9- So give your servant a discerning heart to govern your people and to distinguish between right and wrong. For who is able to govern this great people of yours?

One Another's Mind

When we're both on each others mind
As we struggle with the need to communicate and not whine
Everyone let's pride get in the way
Holding words inside with nothing more to say
No one wants to give in or apologize first
That's when pride gets in the way and the situation
  becomes worse
We're both just guessing as to what's going on
Verses being adults and picking up the phone
Although we are far away the love still remains the same
Holding on to memories stored in a frame
There were some good days
Yes, we both had our ways
The uncontrollable laughs and the silliness that we shared
Although we would fuss we know we both cared
Obstacles tended to come and go
As we tended to go through and not let it show
The weight became heavy every time
As we tried to ignore vs discussing what's on our mind
Just waiting to see what the next steps will be
Trusting God for the rest of my life is the primary key!

Proverbs 17:27 - The one who has knowledge uses words with restraint, and whoever has understanding is even-tempered.

Never Say Never

I always told myself never say never
I said many times I would never go back to school
As I had no desire but just to be relaxed and cool
I attempted school at least three times
fifteen years later I decided to go back and grind
With three kids as my youngest starting kindergarten
And my oldest being a licensed barber
Life appearing to be so complicated
As I've put off school and always hesitated
Taking that first step to just get up and just do it
Here I am after taking the first step, and now I'm all into it
Procrastination is sometimes the biggest thing
For if you go ahead and start it you can end with a bling
It's never too late to get up and elevate
Look at me because I can relate
Don't put off tomorrow for what we can do today
Take advantage of each opportunity
Sometimes they're right within your community
Reach for the stars in your very own way
Go follow your dreams that's all I have to say!

1 Corinthians 2:9-However, as it is written: What no eye has seen, what no ear has heard, and what no human mind has conceived the things God has prepared for those who love him—

Manipulation is Real

Yes, I once thought it was a figure of speech
Until it became a part of life within my own reach
Yes the word manipulation is real
Just them trying to win as if it's a deal
They will fill your head with so much stuff
And you will actually believe and trust
They are only saying it because that's what you want to hear
It's not from their heart they just have your ear
They will always turn the situation around
So it can work in their favor and have you feeling down
Just to have you feeling good at the moment
As they're only building their ego up for the moment
Manipulation can be somewhat like a bribery
As it can happen like a robbery
Robbing you from who you really are
Just to continue on and have you in a war
Robbing you from your true feelings and thought
Just to ignore the situation so they don't get caught
Always remain true to yourself and express how you feel
Not just what they want for you because you will never heal
Manipulation is not for your benefit just theirs alone
Knowing how to use their words and their tone
Trying to get over, beat, and talk their way through
They knowing the entire time they aren't being true
No matter how clever the manipulator may be
God is still watching over both you and me
It may seem they are getting away
But just know God has the last say!

Galatians 5:21 -and envy; drunkenness, orgies, and the like. I warn you, as I did before, that those who live like this will not inherit the kingdom of God.

How are you going to heal
From the inside pain that you feel
You can't continue to hide
As it will only cause damage inside
I will like you to face the pain you feel
As you carry this weight it becomes more real
The burden you carry will impact how you live
Impact the love you show and the love you give
You have to let it go before you want to kill
Mentally killing yourself and others causing an ill
There are many ways to start your journey to heal
First you must acknowledge that things are real
It's ok to be honest and express how you feel
Keeping it inside can become a very big deal
Some need to heal from childhood experiences
As they will always hunt you to cause you reminiscing
Reminiscing on all the hurt and all the pain
And not on how you can move forward and still gain
Being able to move forward
As God always has you covered
That hurt you experienced from words or from a touch
It's still a pain even if others think it's not that much
Don't keep hiding and running from the pain
As the sunshine is coming to break this generational chain
It's hard to help someone if you're not healed yourself
It's like removing a bandaid
Knowing it should have stayed
You must conquer this fear so that you can rest
Not facing it, it will become nothing but stress
I rather you heal much sooner than later
As that weight will grow and become heavier
So let me pause and ask you

Maybe there be one two or three
How will you heal trying to recover from grief
As the enemy try and consume you like a thief
Yes, I know the pain is painful no matter the extent
Get yourself a healing just as it was meant
You still have the victory on this battlefield
It's all up to you and your desired will
No matter if the hurt is from a stranger or even a kin
We can face it so that we can truly smile again
Yes I know it will not be an easy walk
Making the step closer even if it's just having a talk
Healing yourself is really a need
As we can sow into others and help feed their seed
Hiding the pain will try to impact your future
Have you remaining a baby and not getting maturer
Then you can grow in more places than one or two
Healing yourself is something you can do!
Doors will begin to open and so will your mind
Just remain true to yourself and always kind
As only you were created at this appointed time
God knew every challenge you would face
As you were made strong just for this race
You can start healing to accept being a very unique design
As it may not be for everyone as they will remain blind
Healing is just not for others but mainly for you
I want you to try and move forward to do what you do
We all have been scorn in some type of way
It's releasing that hurt in any given day
Some may release by reading or writing
While others may choose by eating and fighting
There is no right or wrong way as you try to release
We just need the unwanted pain to cease
I know there is a pain that no one can see
Just go ahead and face it and set yourself free
Some days you may want to yell and scream
You just wish you can wake up from this unwanted dream

Maybe you lost someone you loved so dearly
And it's stopping you from moving on clearly

It might feel like you're sinking and drowning
But you can heal and keep going and not just frowning
It's like when you take one step forward
Here come three to bring you back
I want you to keep pushing as it's just an attack
An attack from the enemy , as he don't want you free
Give it to the unity the Holy Trinity
Give the enemy a boot in the tail
 and send him straight back to hell
Because you will be healed this day we will tell!

Psalms 147:3-He heals the brokenhearted and binds up their wounds.

H.
Healing

What do you need to be healed from?

____

____

How long have you been hurting from this experience?

____

____

In what way are you willing to start your healing process?

(ex. conversation, writing, speaking up, praying, fasting, dieting, exercising, eating healthy etc.)

____

____

E.
Elevating

What are your goals for the next 1 to 5 years?

____

____

What are some next steps your're going to take to achieve your goal?

____

____

What are you willing to giveup/sacrifice to achieve your goals?
(ex. shopping, hanging out regularly, cooking, sleeping etc.)

____

____

R.
Releasing

What's inside of you that you need to release for you to move forward?
(ex. anger, bitterness, hurt, your past etc.)

Is there anyone you need to release?